A LITTLE

Vi
Pastries

JENI WRIGHT

Illustrated by AISLINN ADAMS

APPLETREE PRESS

First published in 1995 by
The Appletree Press Ltd, 19–21 Alfred Street,
Belfast BT2 8DL
Tel. +44 (0) 1232 243074
Fax +44 (0) 1232 246756
Copyright © 1995 The Appletree Press Ltd.

A Little Book of Viennese Pastries

A catalogue record for this book is
available from the British Library.

ISBN 0-86281-539-8

9 8 7 6 5 4 3 2 1

For my children, Oliver and Sophie

Introduction

Is it any wonder that from a city as elegant and beautiful as Vienna should come such a wonderful array of cakes and pastries? This city of literally thousands of pastry shops and coffee houses has a long and illustrious tradition of baking. For the Viennese, eating cakes and pastries is one of life's richest – and oldest – pleasures.

It began over five hundred years ago, when Emperor Frederick V of Austria ordered bread rolls to be stamped with his likeness. It seems that from then on Austrian bakers never looked back. Over the centuries, and particularly in the days when Vienna was the capital of the vast and wealthy Austro-Hungarian Empire, more and more recipes for exquisite cakes, breads and pastries were created; Viennese bakers vied with each other over whose were the best. Cakes which are now world-famous, such as *Sachertorte* and *Doboztorte*, were invented in Vienna; so too was *Apfelstrudel* and the distinctively shaped *Gugelhupf*, not to mention an incredible number of chocolate gâteaux, nut cakes and fresh fruit tarts.

The coffee houses of Vienna are still filled today with customers lingering over a coffee and enjoying a pastry – and maybe indulging themselves in an extra helping of *Schlagobers*, the famous whipped cream so beloved by the Viennese. In this *Little Book of Viennese Pastries*, you will find many of the famous Viennese specialities, plus some lesser known but no less delicious recipes of the kind made at home. *Guten Appetit!*

A note on measures
Measurements are given in imperial, metric and American measurements. It is important not to mix the three, but to stick to only one in any one recipe. Spoon measurements are level unless otherwise indicated.

Vanilla Crescents

Vanillekipferl

These sweet little biscuits were traditionally a Christmas speciality, but nowadays they are baked all year round. Take care when baking them that they do not brown – they should be pale in colour so that they taste light and buttery. If overbaked, they become brittle and will taste singed.

Pastry:	1 egg yolk
5 oz/125g/1¼ cups plain flour	pinch of salt
4 oz/100g/½ cup unsalted	2 tsp vanilla sugar
butter, softened	**To finish:**
1½ oz/40g/3 tbsp icing sugar	2 oz/50g/⅓ cup icing sugar
2 oz/50g/½ cup ground almonds	2 tsp vanilla sugar
(makes about 25)	

Pre-heat oven to gas mark 4/350°F/180°C. Put all ingredients in a bowl and knead with your hands to a firm dough. Cover and chill for 1 hour.

Break off walnut-sized pieces of dough and roll each piece into a sausage shape about 2½ in/6 cm long. Form into about 25 crescent shapes with tapered ends.

Put the crescents on a greased and floured baking sheet and bake for 20–25 minutes. Sift the icing and vanilla sugars onto a plate. Take the crescents from the oven and immediately roll them in the sugar mixture. Place on a rack and sprinkle with the remaining sugar. Leave to cool before serving.

Note Make vanilla sugar by keeping a vanilla pod in a jar of caster sugar. Use as needed.

The Emperor's Gugelhupf

Kaisergugelhupf

Gugelhupf is said to have been made originally for the Emperor
Franz Joseph I. There are many different versions, some made with
yeast, some quite plain without the raisins and almonds, and others
with a liberal coating of icing sugar. This version is quick and simple
because it is made with baking powder. The chocolate icing gives
it a luxurious finishing touch.

Pastry:	4 eggs
4 oz/100g/³/₄ cup raisins	7¹/₂ oz/225g/1³/₄ cups plain flour
2–3 tbsp rum	2 tsp baking powder
7 oz/200g/1 cup unsalted butter, softened	3 oz/75g/³/₄ cup flaked or chopped almonds
7 oz/200g/1 cup caster sugar	**Icing:**
1 tbsp vanilla sugar (see p. 4)	7 oz/200g plain chocolate, chopped
finely grated zest of 1 lemon	a knob of butter
pinch of salt	
(serves 12–14)	

Pre-heat oven to gas mark 4/350°F/180°C. Soak the raisins in the
rum for about 10 minutes. Beat together the butter, sugars, lemon
zest and salt until light and fluffy. Beat in the eggs one at a time, then
beat in the flour sifted with the baking powder. Carefully fold in
the raisins and rum with the almonds. Pour into a greased and
floured 2 pint/1 litre/5-cup *Gugelhupf* tin and bake for about 50
minutes until springy to the touch. Invert onto a rack. To make
the icing: Melt the chocolate and butter in a bowl over a pan of hot
water, then immediately spread it over the cake while the cake is
still warm. Leave to cool before serving.

Austrian Applecake

Österreichischer Apfelkuchen

Although always described as a cake, this is in fact a large sweet tart with a gooey apple filling. Any dessert apples can be used, but Golden Delicious are especially good. Be sure to spread the icing over the top of the cake as soon as the cake comes out of the oven. If the cake is left to go cold before it is iced, the icing will crack.

Pastry:	$^1/_2$ tsp vanilla sugar (see p. 4)
7 oz/200g/1$^1/_2$ cups plain flour	$^1/_2$ tsp rum
4 oz/100g/$^1/_2$ cup caster sugar	4 oz/100g/1 cup chopped or
4 oz/100g/$^1/_2$ cup unsalted	flaked almonds
butter, cut into pieces	finely grated zest and juice of
1 egg, beaten	1 lemon
$^1/_2$ tsp ground cinnamon	1 tbsp seedless raspberry jam
Filling:	**Icing:**
1lb/450g dessert apples	6 oz/150g/1 cup icing sugar
4 oz/100g/$^1/_2$ cup caster sugar	2 tbsp lemon juice
4 fl oz/125ml/$^1/_2$ cup water	$^1/_2$ egg white
(serves 10–12)	

Pre-heat oven to gas mark 6/400°F/200°C. To make the pastry: Put all ingredients in a bowl and mix with your hands to make a firm dough. Chill for 30 minutes. Peel and core the apples, then cut into small dice. Put the caster sugar in a pan with the water, vanilla sugar and rum. Bring to the boil, then add the apples, almonds and lemon zest and juice. Simmer gently, stirring frequently, for about 30 minutes or until the apples are soft and jelly like. Leave to cool. Roll out the dough on a lightly floured surface and use to line an 11 in/28 cm fluted-edged flan tin. Prick dough with a fork, then spread with

8

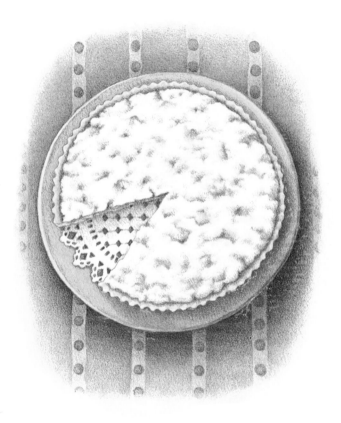

the jam and spoon in the cold apple filling. Bake for 30 minutes.

To make the icing: Mix the icing sugar with the lemon juice and egg white, then spread over the top of the warm cake. Leave to cool before serving.

Plum Cake with Cinnamon Streusel

Pflaumenkuchen mit Zimtstreusel

This cake has a yeasted base rather like a sweet pizza dough, and a wonderfully moist plum topping. Arrange the plums on the dough like little canoes with their skins facing downwards. This way, the juice from the plums will not seep into the dough and make it soggy.

1lb/450g/4 cups plain flour	2lb/1kg red plums,
pinch of salt	preferably Victoria
2 tbsp dried yeast	**Streusel topping:**
3½ oz/90g/⅓ cup caster sugar	6 oz/150g/1½ cups plain flour
8 fl oz/250ml/1 cup lukewarm milk	4 oz/100g/½ cup unsalted butter, cut into pieces
4 oz/100g/½ cup unsalted butter, softened	2 oz/50g/¼ cup caster sugar
	1 tsp ground cinnamon
(makes about 20 squares)	

Sift the flour and salt into a bowl, make a well in the centre and put in the yeast. Add 1 tablespoon of the sugar and 5 tablespoons of the milk to the well and mix with the yeast to make a batter. Leave for 5 minutes.

Flake the butter into the bowl, sprinkle in the remaining sugar, then add the remaining milk and knead with your hands to make a smooth, elastic dough. Leave to rise in a warm place for about 1 hour or until almost doubled in size. Meanwhile, halve and stone the plums, then cut each half in half or quarters depending on their size. Pre-heat oven to gas mark 6/400°F/200°C. Roll out the dough on a lightly floured surface and use to line a buttered 17 x 14 in/43 x 35 cm baking tray. Arrange the plum pieces, skin side down, on the dough. Mix together the streusel ingredients and sprinkle over the plums. Bake for 30–40 minutes until the base is golden and the plums cooked through. Serve warm or cold, cut into squares.

Raspberry Cream Roulade

Himbeerroulade

This is a large cake for a special occasion. The cake itself is light and airy, while the typically Austrian filling of Quark, Chantilly cream and fresh raspberries lightly set with gelatine is luxuriously rich.

6 eggs, separated	2 oz/50g/¼ cup caster sugar
100g/4 oz/¹/₂ cup caster sugar	1 oz/25g/1 tbsp vanilla sugar
2 tbsp vanilla sugar (see p. 4)	(see p. 4)
pinch of salt	1 sachet gelatine powder
5 oz/120g/1¼ cups plain flour	7 oz/200g/1 scant cup Quark
Filling:	10 oz/300g/2 cups fresh
whites of 3 eggs	raspberries
4 fl oz/125ml/¹/₂ cup whipping cream	1–2 tbsp icing sugar

(serves 12)

To make the cake: Pre-heat oven to gas mark 7/425°F/220°C. Beat the egg whites with 2 tablespoons of the sugar until stiff. In another bowl, mix the egg yolks with the remaining sugar, vanilla sugar and salt

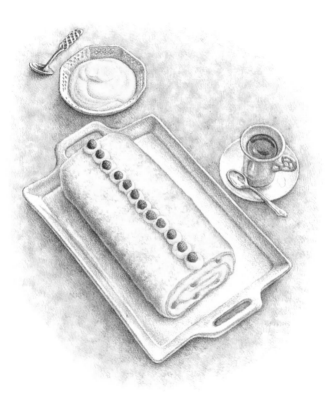

until creamy. Fold in the beaten egg whites and then the flour a spoonful at a time. Spread in a greased and lined 17 x 14 in/43 x 35 cm baking tray and bake for 10–12 minutes until springy to the touch.

Immediately invert the cake onto a sheet of greaseproof paper sprinkled with caster sugar. Starting at one end, carefully rub a dampened cloth over the lining paper and peel the paper away from the cake as you rub. While the cake is still warm, carefully roll it up from one of the long ends. Leave to cool, seam side down.

To make the filling: Beat the egg whites until stiff. Whip the cream with the sugars and fold in the beaten egg whites. Dissolve the gelatine in 4 tablespoons water according to packet instructions, then blend into the Quark. Fold the whipped cream into the Quark. Unroll the *roulade*. Reserve a little of the Quark filling for the decoration, then spread the remainder over the *roulade*. Dot with the raspberries, reserving 12 for decoration. Leave the filling for about 10 minutes until just beginning to set, then roll up the *roulade* as before. Sift over the icing sugar, then pipe 12 little rounds with the reserved Quark filling in a line on top and put a raspberry in the centre of each one. Keep in a cold place until serving time. Cut into slices with a hot knife.

Little Nut Horns

Nußbeugel

With their gooey, nutty filling and sweet rich dough, these little pastries are so unbelievably good that you may very well find they disappear within minutes of being taken out of the oven.

Pastry:	**Filling:**
7 oz/200g/1¾ cups plain flour	4 oz/100g blanched almonds
3 oz/75g/⅓ cup unsalted butter, softened	4 oz/100g walnut halves
1 oz/25g/2 tbsp icing sugar	4 oz/100g shelled and skinned hazelnuts
2 tsp dried yeast	3 oz/90g/½ cup icing sugar
1 egg yolk	1 oz/25g/2 tbsp unsalted butter
3 tbsp milk	4 fl oz/125ml/½ cup milk
pinch of salt	2 tbsp vanilla sugar
1 egg yolk mixed with a little egg white, to glaze	1 tsp ground cinnamon

(makes 10)

To make the pastry: Put all the ingredients in a bowl and mix with your hands. Gather into a ball and leave to rest for about 30 minutes. Meanwhile, grind all the nuts together in a food processor. Bring the remaining filling ingredients to a boil in a heavy pan. Stir in the nuts and boil, stirring constantly, until the mixture becomes a thick and creamy mass. Leave to cool.

Divide the dough into 10 equal pieces and roll each piece into a sausage shape about 7 in/18 cm long and 4 in/10 cm wide. Put 2 heaped tablespoons filling in the centre of each piece of dough, leaving a 1 in/2.5 cm border all around. Fold in the sides over the filling and press to seal, then place the pieces of dough on a greased baking sheet and form into horseshoe shapes with the seams in the centre. Fold in the ends to seal in the filling completely.

Brush the nut horns with the egg glaze and leave to rest for about 30 minutes in a cool place. Meanwhile, pre-heat oven to gas mark 5/375°F/190°C. Brush again with egg glaze, then bake for 20 minutes. Serve warm or cold.

Raspberry and Almond Tartlets

Ischler Törtchen

These sweet little tartlets are named after Bad Ischl, where Emperor Franz Josef had his summer residence. Traditionally they are round in shape, but these star shapes look much prettier, and are ideal for a Christmas treat. You can, of course, make them any shape you like.

---

6 oz/150g/1½ cups plain flour
2 oz/50g/½ cup ground almonds
3 oz/75g/½ cup icing sugar
2 tbsp vanilla sugar (see p. 4)

pinch of salt
5 oz/120g/⅔ cup unsalted
butter, softened
2–3 tbsp raspberry jam

(makes 20)

Mix all the ingredients except the jam and knead until firm. Chill for about 30 minutes. Meanwhile, pre-heat oven to gas mark 4/ 350°F/180°C. Roll the dough out on a floured surface until about ⅛ in/3 mm thick. The dough will be very sticky so make sure that the surface and rolling pin are well floured. Cut out 40 star shapes using a small biscuit cutter, then cut out a tiny hole in the centre of half the stars. Put all the stars on greased and floured baking sheets and bake for about 8 minutes or until just light golden. Do not let the stars get brown. Sift icing sugar over the stars with the holes in while they are still warm. Leave to cool. Spread jam on the stars without holes, spreading it more generously in the centre, then press the other stars carefully on top, with the icing sugar facing outwards. The jam will peep through the holes.

Viennese Nut Cake

Wiener Nußkuchen

Recipes for nut cakes can be found all over Austria. This one from Vienna is made with ground hazelnuts. It has fresh breadcrumbs in the batter which give the cake a light texture.

---

7 oz/200g/1 cup unsalted butter, softened	3 tbsp apricot jam
	1½ tbsp water
7 oz/200g/1 cup caster sugar	**Icing:**
1½ tbsp vanilla sugar (see p. 4)	4 oz/100g/½ cup caster sugar
4 eggs	4 oz/100g plain chocolate, chopped
7 oz/200g/1¾ cups plain flour	
2 oz/50g/1 cup fresh breadcrumbs	1 oz/25g/2 tbsp unsalted butter, softened
2 tsp baking powder	2 tbsp water
3 tsp cocoa powder	10–12 whole hazelnuts, to decorate
6 oz/150g/1⅔ cups ground hazelnuts	

(serves 10–12)

Pre-heat oven to gas mark 4/350°F/180°C. Beat the butter, sugars and eggs with an electric mixer until creamy. Add the flour, breadcrumbs, baking powder and cocoa powder and mix until smooth, then add the hazelnuts. Turn the mixture into a greased and floured 2 pint/1 litre/5 cup *Gugelhupf* tin and bake for 50–60 minutes or until a skewer inserted in the cake comes out clean. Leave to cool in the tin for 10 minutes, then invert onto a plate. Melt the jam with the water in a small pan, work through a sieve, then brush over the cake. Leave to cool.

Put all the icing ingredients in a pan and heat until smooth. Pour over the cake and spread with a knife while still warm. Decorate with the whole hazelnuts and leave to set before serving.

Christmas Butter Cookies

Weihnachtsgebäck

It is traditional for Austrian families to make special cookies for Christmas, and many families have their own recipe which is passed down from generation to generation.

---

5 oz/120g/²⁄₃ cup unsalted butter, softened	2 tbsp vanilla sugar (see p. 4)
3 oz/75g/¹⁄₂ cup icing sugar	1 egg yolk mixed with
1 egg yolk	1 tbsp water
8 oz/250g/2 cups plain flour	a few tbsp chopped nuts
(makes about 40)	

Pre-heat oven to gas mark 6/400°F/200°C. Mix the butter, sugar and egg yolk together with your hands. Add the flour and vanilla sugar and knead to a firm dough. Chill for about 2 hours. Roll out the dough on a floured surface until about ¹⁄₄ in/5 mm thick. Cut out about 40 Christmas shapes such as stars, bells, Father Christmas, angels, holly leaves, etc., either freehand or with the appropriate biscuit cutters. Place the biscuits on baking sheets lined with non-stick baking parchment, brush with the egg glaze and sprinkle with nuts. Bake for 8–10 minutes or until lightly coloured. Leave to cool on racks before serving.

Marble Cake

Marmorkuchen

This is a plain tea-time cake with a difference – white and chocolate mixtures marbled together. Everyone is always intrigued as to how it's done, and yet it's unbelievably simple – once you know how. Serve it sliced, to reveal the pretty marbled effect.

---

7 oz/200g/1 cup unsalted butter, softened	pinch of salt
7 oz/200g/1 cup caster sugar	4 eggs
2 tbsp vanilla sugar (see p. 4)	4 fl oz/125 ml/¹/₂ cup milk
10 oz/300g/2¹/₂ cups plain flour	3 tbsp cocoa powder
2 tsp baking powder	icing sugar, to decorate

(serves 8–10)

Pre-heat oven to gas mark 6/400°F/200°C. Beat the butter and sugars with an electric mixer until light and fluffy. Sift the flour with the baking powder and salt. Beat the eggs one at a time into the creamed mixture, adding a little of the flour mixture with the last egg if the mixture shows signs of curdling.

Fold in the flour mixture, then stir in 2–4 tablespoons of the milk to make a creamy batter. Put two-thirds of the batter into a greased and floured 2 pint/1 litre/5-cup *Gugelhupf* tin.

Stir the cocoa powder into the remaining batter, then add the remaining milk. This batter should be much thinner and runnier than the plain one in the tin. Pour the dark batter into the tin and swirl it carefully into the plain batter with a knife. Bake for 50–60 minutes until a skewer inserted in the cake comes out clean. Leave to cool for about 20 minutes, then invert onto a rack and leave to cool completely. Dust with icing sugar before serving.

Carnival Jam Doughnuts

Faschingskrapfen

These doughnuts date back to the early seventeenth century, when they were first made in Vienna for the Fasching celebrations in January and February leading up to Shrove Tuesday (the last day before Lent).

---

10 oz/300g/2¹/₂ cups plain flour	1 egg
1 tbsp dried yeast	1 egg yolk
2 tsp caster sugar	2 oz/50g/¹/₄ cup unsalted butter,
4 tbsp lukewarm milk	melted and cooled
1 tbsp vanilla sugar (see p. 4)	4 tbsp apricot or raspberry jam
¹/₂ tsp ground cinnamon	vegetable oil for deep-frying
pinch of salt	caster sugar, to decorate
(makes 12–14)	

Mix two-thirds of the flour with the yeast, 1 teaspoon of the caster sugar and the milk. Leave to rise for about 20 minutes in a warm place. Add the remaining sugar, vanilla sugar, cinnamon, salt, egg, egg yolk and butter. Beat together until bubbles form on the surface of the batter, then add the remaining flour and knead with your hands until you have a smooth and elastic dough which is not sticky. Leave to rise in a warm place for another 20 minutes.

Roll out the dough on a floured surface until ¹/₄ in/5 mm thick, then cut into 24–28 round shapes with the rim of a 2¹/₂ in/6 cm glass. Put a little spot of jam in the centre of half the rounds, then cover with the remaining rounds and press the edges together to seal. Press the rim of the glass over the doughnuts again and cut off any uneven edges. Deep-fry the doughnuts in batches in about ¹/₂ in/ 1 cm of hot oil for a few minutes or until golden brown on each side.

Remove from the oil with a slotted spoon and drain on a rack, then roll in caster sugar before serving. Serve as fresh as possible.

Almond Kisses

Mandelküsse

These pretty little sweetmeats make good *petits fours* to serve with coffee and liqueurs at the end of a dinner party.

---

5 oz/125g/²/₃ cup unsalted butter, softened	2 egg yolks
3 oz/75g/¹/₃ cup caster sugar, plus 1 tbsp	1 egg white, lightly beaten
2 tbsp vanilla sugar	5 oz/125g/1¹/₃ cups ground almonds
7 oz/200g/1³/₄ cups plain flour	2 tbsp seedless raspberry jam

(makes about 40)

Pre-heat oven to gas mark 4/350°F/180°C. Beat the butter, 3 oz/75g/¹/₃ cup caster sugar, vanilla sugar and egg yolks with an electric mixer until light and fluffy. Sift in the flour and knead quickly with your hands to a firm dough.

Form the dough into about 40 nut-sized balls, roll in the beaten egg white and then in the almonds. Put them on greased baking sheets and make small indentations in the top of each ball with the handle of a teaspoon. Fill the indentations with jam, then sprinkle the balls with the 1 tbsp caster sugar. Bake for 15–20 minutes. Leave to cool before serving.

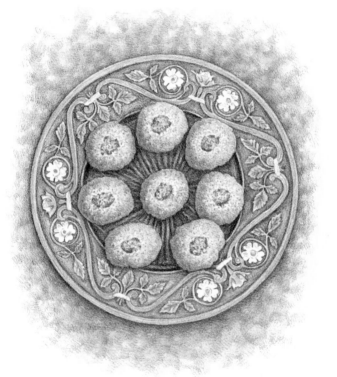

Viennese Fingers

Wiener Plätzchen

These delightful little biscuits are perhaps one of the best-known Viennese pastries outside Austria. You can buy them commercially made, but they are very quick and easy to make and the homemade ones taste fresher.

---

8 oz/250g/1 cup unsalted butter, softened
2 oz/50g/¹/₃ cup icing sugar
a few drops of vanilla essence
8 oz/250g/2 cups self-raising flour
4 oz/100g plain chocolate, chopped
(makes about 20)

Pre-heat oven to gas mark 5/375°F/190°C. Beat the butter, icing sugar and vanilla essence until pale and creamy. Sift in the flour and beat again until evenly mixed. Pipe the mixture with a star nozzle on to buttered baking sheets, making about 20 x 3 in/7.5 cm fingers. Space them well apart because they spread during baking. Bake for 10–15 minutes, then cool slightly, then transfer to racks and leave until cold. Melt the chocolate in a bowl over a pan of hot water. Remove the bowl from the pan and dip both ends of each finger in the melted chocolate. Return to the racks and leave until set before serving.

Drum Cake

Doboztorte

This classic layer cake can be seen in *pâtisseries* all over Austria. It is quite difficult to make at home, but well worth the effort if you have the time to spare. If you don't have six baking sheets, mark the circles on six sheets of paper as instructed in the recipe, but bake the cake layers in batches according to how many baking sheets you have.

Cake:
4 eggs, size 2
6 oz/175g/³/₄ cup caster sugar
5 oz/150g/1¹/₄ cups plain flour
pinch of salt
3 oz/75g hazelnuts, toasted and finely chopped

Chocolate cream:
8 oz/250g/1 cup unsalted butter, softened
3 oz/75g/¹/₂ cup icing sugar
8 oz/250g plain chocolate, melted
1 egg yolk

Caramel:
5 oz/150g/²/₃ cup granulated sugar

Pre-heat oven to gas mark 5/375°F/190°C. Line six baking sheets with non-stick baking parchment and mark an 8 in/20 cm circle on each sheet. Put the eggs and sugar in a large bowl over a pan of hot water and beat with a whisk until very thick and pale and the beaters leave a ribbon trail when lifted. Remove the bowl from the pan and continue whisking until the mixture is cold. Sift in the flour and salt and fold in gently with a large metal spoon. Spread the mixture on the marked circles, then bake for 5–6 minutes. As soon as the rounds come out of the oven, transfer them to racks and peel off paper when just cool. To make the chocolate cream: Beat the butter and sugar until pale and creamy, then beat in the melted chocolate and egg yolk. Sandwich five cake layers together with the

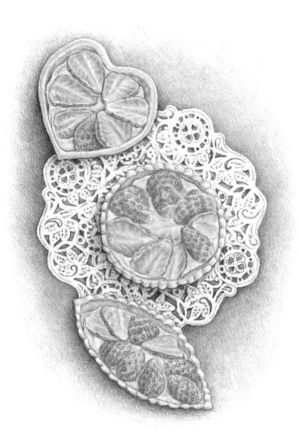

together with the chocolate cream and spread it on the top and sides. Press the chopped hazelnuts into the side.

Put the remaining cake layer on a lightly oiled baking sheet. Melt the granulated sugar in a heavy pan until it thickens and turns a golden caramel colour, then immediately pour over the cake layer. Let the caramel cool a little then cut into 12 portions with sharp scissors. Leave until cold, then place on top of the cake. If there is any chocolate cream left over, it can be used to pipe rosettes around the top edge of the cake.

Little Strawberry Tarts

Erdbeertörtchen

According to the whim of the chef, these little tarts may come in many different shapes.

Pastry:	2 egg yolks
4 oz/100g/1 cup plain flour	**Filling:**
pinch of salt	8 oz/250g/1 cup cream cheese
2 oz/50g/¼ cup unsalted butter, chilled	juice of 1 lemon
4 oz/100g/½ cup caster sugar	5 tbsp redcurrant jelly
finely grated zest of 1 lemon	8 oz/250g/1⅓ cups strawberries, hulled and sliced
(makes 12)	

To make the pastry: Sift the flour and salt into a bowl. Add the butter in pieces and work with the fingertips until the mixture resembles breadcrumbs. Stir in half the sugar and the lemon zest, then add the egg yolks and mix with your fingertips until the dough draws together. Gather into a ball and chill for 30 minutes.

Roll out the dough on a floured surface and cut out shapes to line 12 individual tartlet moulds. Prick the dough and chill for 30 minutes. Meanwhile, pre-heat oven to gas mark 5/375°F/190°C. Line the dough with foil and fill with baking beans. Bake blind for 15 minutes, remove the foil and beans and bake for a further 3 minutes or until the pastry is crisp and golden. Leave to cool. Beat the cream cheese with the remaining sugar and half the lemon juice. Remove the pastry shells from the moulds. Melt the redcurrant jelly with the remaining lemon juice and brush inside the pastry shells. Fill with the cream cheese, then arrange the strawberry slices decoratively on top and brush with the remaining redcurrant jelly. Leave to set before serving.

Apricot and Chocolate Rolls

Rogalach

Originally from a Jewish recipe, these croissant-shaped pastries are absolutely divine, especially when served still warm from the oven.

5 oz/150g/1¼ cups plain flour	5–6 tbsp apricot jam
pinch of salt	2 oz/50g plain chocolate chips
4 oz/125g/½ cup unsalted butter, chilled	melted butter to glaze
3 fl oz/75 ml/scant ⅓ cup Quark	icing sugar to garnish
(makes 16)	

Pre-heat oven to gas mark 5/375°F/190°C. To make the pastry: Sift the flour and salt into a bowl. Add the butter in pieces and work with the fingertips until the mixture resembles breadcrumbs. Stir in the Quark and gather the dough together with your fingertips.

Divide the dough in half, wrap each piece in foil and chill for 1 hour.

Roll 1 piece of dough out on a floured surface to roughly an 8 in/20 cm round. Cut the round into 8 triangular wedges. Spread apricot jam on each wedge and then sprinkle with a few chocolate chips. Roll up from the curved edge so that the pointed end is on top. Repeat with the remaining piece of dough and the jam and chocolate. Arrange the rolls on buttered baking sheets and brush with melted butter. Bake for about 15–20 minutes until golden. Sprinkle with icing sugar while still hot.

Sachertorte

This most famous of all Viennese cakes was invented in 1832 by Franz Sacher, chef to Prince Metternich.

---

4 oz/100g/¹/₂ cup unsalted butter, softened	**Icing:** 8 oz/250g plain chocolate, chopped
3 oz/75g/¹/₂ cup icing sugar	
4 oz/100g plain chocolate, melted	2 oz/50g/¹/₄ cup vanilla sugar (see p. 4)
5 eggs, separated	
3 oz/75g/¹/₃ cup caster sugar	6 oz/150g/1 cup icing sugar
3 oz/75g/³/₄ cup plain flour	3¹/₂ fl oz/100ml/scant ¹/₂ cup water
Glaze:	
4 tbsp apricot jam	
2 tbsp water	
(serves 10–12)	

Pre-heat oven to gas mark 4/350°F/180°C. Beat the butter and icing sugar with an electric mixer until light and fluffy. Beat in the melted chocolate and egg yolks. Whisk the egg whites and caster sugar until stiff, then fold into the butter and sugar mixture. Sift and fold in the flour in 3 batches. Pour into a greased and lined 9 in/ 23 cm springform tin and bake for 1 hour or until a skewer inserted in the centre comes out clean. Lift off and discard any crisp crust. Leave the cake to cool in the tin, then turn out and remove the lining paper.

To make the glaze: Melt the jam with the water in a pan, then work through a sieve and brush over the top and sides of the cake.

To make the icing: Heat three-quarters of the chocolate in a pan with all the other icing ingredients, stirring constantly. Leave to cool slightly, then pour over the top of the cake and spread over the top and sides with a palette knife. Leave to set. Melt the remaining chocolate and use it to pipe the word "Sacher" on the top of the cake from a greaseproof paper piping bag.

Apple Strudel

Apfelstrudel

Viennese *Apfelstrudel* is famous all over the world, but few people realize that the Viennese borrowed the idea for paper-thin leaves of pastry from the Hungarians, who in turn took it from the Turks.

	Filling:
12 sheets of frozen filo pastry, thawed	2lb/1kg cooking apples
8 oz/250g/1 cup unsalted butter, melted and cooled	finely grated zest and juice of 1 lemon
3 oz/75g/¾ cup ground almonds	3 oz/75g/1 cup raisins
icing sugar, to finish	3 oz/75g/⅓ cup caster sugar
	½ tsp ground cinnamon

(serves 8–10)

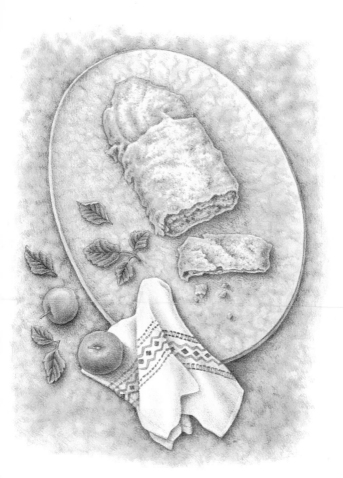

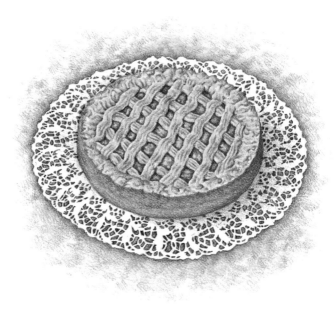

Pre-heat oven to gas mark 6/400°F/200°C. To make the filling: Peel, core and thinly slice the apples and immediately toss them with the other filling ingredients. Dredge a tea towel with flour and place one sheet of filo on it with one of the longest sides facing you. Brush the filo with melted butter. Place another sheet of filo on top of the first and brush with more melted butter. Continue in this way until there are 12 sheets of filo on top of each other with butter in between. Sprinkle the top sheet of buttered filo with the ground almonds, then evenly cover with the filling, leaving a wide border all around the edges. Fold in these edges to seal in the filling, then brush them with melted butter. Using the tea towel to help you, roll up the filo around the filling, starting at the long edge facing you and working away from you. Carefully lift the roll, seam side down, onto a buttered large baking sheet and tuck in the ends so the filling does not ooze out during baking. Brush all over with melted butter and bake for 30 minutes or until crisp and golden. Serve warm, dusted with icing sugar.

Raspberry Tart from Linz

Linzertorte

Pastry:	2¹/₂ oz/65g/scant ¹/₃ cup
6 oz/175g/1¹/₂ cups plain flour	caster sugar
pinch of salt	1 egg, beaten
2 oz/50g/¹/₄ cup unsalted butter, chilled	4 tbsp redcurrant jelly, to glaze
	Filling:
2¹/₂ oz/65g/²/₃ cup ground almonds	12 oz/375g/2¹/₃ cups raspberries
	8 oz/250g/1¹/₄ cups caster sugar
	2 tbsp arrowroot

(serves 6)

To make the pastry: Sift the flour and salt into a bowl. Add the butter and work with the fingertips until the mixture resembles breadcrumbs, then stir in the almonds and sugar. Add the egg and mix with your fingertips until the dough draws together. Gather into a ball and chill for 30 minutes.

Meanwhile, make the filling: put the raspberries and sugar in a heavy pan and stir over moderate heat until the sugar has dissolved. Increase the heat and bring to the boil, then simmer, stirring frequently, for 15–20 minutes or until the mixture looks like thin jam. Mix the arrowroot to a paste with 2 tablespoons water and stir into the raspberry mixture. Stir until the mixture thickens, then remove from the heat and leave to cool.

Set aside a small ball of dough to make the lattice, then roll out the remaining dough and use to line the bottom and sides of an 8 in/ 20 cm flan tin. Chill for 15 minutes.

Pre-heat oven to gas mark 5/375°F/190°C. Spread the cool filling in the tart shell, then roll out the reserved dough and cut out 8 thin strips. Place the strips over the filling in a lattice pattern, sticking them to the edge with a little water. Bake for 35 minutes. Leave the tart to cool in the tin, then warm the redcurrant jelly until melted and brush all over the top. Leave to set before serving.

Chocolate and Hazelnut Tart

Schokoladen-Haselnuß Torte

Chocolate and hazelnuts are two favourite ingredients of the Viennese. Here they are combined together to make a rich, moist tart. Serve it with *Schlagobers* (whipped cream).

Pastry:	Filling:
7 oz/200g/1¾ cups plain flour	3 oz/75g/⅓ cup unsalted butter,
pinch of salt	softened
5 oz/125g/⅔ cup unsalted	5 oz/150g/⅔ cup caster sugar
butter, chilled	2 eggs, beaten
2½ oz/65g/scant ⅓ cup	1 tbsp plain flour
caster sugar	7 oz/200g/2 cups ground hazelnuts
1 egg, beaten	3 oz/75g plain chocolate, grated
grated chocolate, to decorate	2 tbsp brandy or rum

(serves 8–10)

To make the pastry: Sift the flour and salt into a bowl. Add the butter and work with the fingertips until the mixture resembles breadcrumbs, then stir in the sugar. Add the egg and mix with your fingertips until the dough draws together. Gather into a ball, then roll out on a floured surface and use to line a 10 in/25 cm flan tin. Prick the bottom and chill for 30 minutes.

Pre-heat oven to gas mark 6/400°F/200°C. To make the filling: Beat the butter and sugar until light and fluffy, then beat in the eggs and flour followed by the hazelnuts, chocolate and brandy or rum. Put the filling in the tart shell and bake for 25–30 minutes or until the filling is set. Leave to cool in the tin. Serve lukewarm, sprinkled with grated chocolate.

Chocolate Truffle Cake

Trüffeltorte

Every *pâtisserie* has its own recipe for chocolate truffle cake, some exceptionally rich and ornate, others more modest. It's all a question of personal taste as to which you like best. This one is rich and dark, with a very chocolatey *ganache* filling in the centre. It is best to cut into thin slices when serving.

Cake:	12 fl oz/375ml/1 1/2 cups
5 oz/120g/2/3 cup unsalted	double cream
butter, softened	2 tbsp brandy
3 1/2 oz/90g/1/2 cup icing sugar	**Icing:**
5 oz/120g plain chocolate, melted	7 oz/200g/1 cup caster sugar
6 eggs, separated	7 fl oz/200 ml/scant 1 cup water
3 1/2 oz/90g/1/2 cup caster sugar	7 oz/200g plain chocolate,
3 1/2 oz/90g/1 cup plain flour	chopped
Ganache:	frosted rose petals, to decorate
12 oz/375g plain chocolate,	
chopped	

(serves 15)

Pre-heat oven to gas mark 4/350°F/180°C. Beat the butter and icing sugar with an electric mixer until light and fluffy. Beat in the melted chocolate and egg yolks. Whisk the egg whites and caster sugar until stiff, then fold into the butter and sugar mixture. Sift and fold in the flour in 3 batches.

Turn into a greased and lined 9 in/23 cm springform tin and bake for 1 hour or until a skewer inserted in the centre comes out clean. Leave the cake to cool in the tin, then turn it out and remove the lining paper. Cut the cake horizontally in half and return one half to the tin.

To make the *ganache*: Put the chopped chocolate in a bowl. Heat the cream until very hot, then pour over the chocolate and stir until the chocolate has melted and the mixture is smooth. Stir in the brandy and leave to cool, then beat with the electric mixer until fluffy. Spread the *ganache* on top of the cake layer in the tin, then put the second cake layer on top. Chill for 1 hour.

To make the icing: Put the sugar and water in a heavy pan, heat gently until the sugar has dissolved, then boil without stirring until a white syrup is formed (do not allow it to colour). Add the chocolate and continue boiling until the icing is thick, then pour over the top of the cake and spread evenly over the top and sides. Chill for at least 4 hours before serving decorated with frosted rose petals.

Chocolate Truffles

Schokoladentrüffel

If you have any stale leftover Christmas cake, or even cold Christmas pudding, these truffles are an ideal way to use it up.

4 oz/100g rich fruit cake, crumbled	2 oz/50g/¹/₃ cup icing sugar
4 oz/100g/1¹/₄ cups ground almonds	4 oz/100g plain chocolate, melted
	2 tbsp rum
	cocoa powder, for coating
(makes about 25)	

Mix the cake crumbs, ground almonds and sugar and stir well. Mix in the chocolate and rum. Knead until the mixture comes together, then shape into about 25 balls and roll in cocoa powder. Chill before serving.

Bishop's Bread

Bischofsbrot

This Christmas speciality is traditionally baked in a *Rehrücken* mould, which gives it its characteristic barrel shape.

---

5 eggs, separated
4 oz/100g/½ cup caster sugar
1½ oz/40g/3 tbsp unsalted butter, softened
4 oz/100g/1 cup plain flour, sifted
2 oz/50g/½ cup flaked almonds
2 oz/50g/⅓ cup sultanas
2 oz/50g/½ cup dried apricots, finely chopped
2 oz/50g/½ cup candied mixed peel, finely chopped
(serves about 8)

Pre-heat oven to gas mark 4/350°F/180°C. Beat the egg yolks, sugar and butter with an electric mixer until creamy. Beat in the flour, then the nuts and fruits.

Whisk the egg whites until stiff, then fold into the batter until evenly incorporated. Turn into a greased and floured 1¾ pint/1 litre/4½-cup *Rehrücken* mould or Balmoral cake tin and bake for 40–45 minutes or until a skewer inserted in the centre comes out clean. Invert onto a rack and leave to cool before serving.

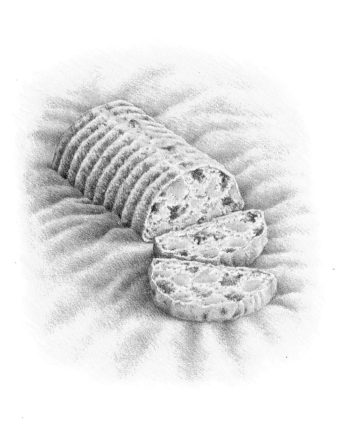

Cherry Cream Slices

Kirschcremeschnitten

Layers of crisp, light puff pastry, rich *crème pâtissière*, sweet ripe cherries and kirsch make luscious melt-in-the-mouth pastries.

2 egg yolks	8 oz/250g frozen puff pastry,
2 oz/50g/¼ cup caster sugar	thawed
2 oz/50g/½ cup cornflour	½ pt/300ml/1¼ cups double
½ pt/300ml/1¼ cups milk	cream
2 tbsp kirsch	1lb/450g/2⅔ cups cherries

(serves 6)

Pre-heat oven to gas mark 7/425°F/220°C. Mix the egg yolks, sugar and cornflour in a bowl. Scald the milk in a pan, then stir into the egg yolk mixture. Return to the pan and simmer, stirring, until thick. Remove from the heat and stir in the kirsch. Cover the surface of the custard with cling film and leave to cool.

Roll out the pastry on a floured surface to a 14 x 12 in/35 x 30 cm rectangle. Place on a wetted baking sheet, prick all over with a fork and bake for 10 minutes. Carefully ease the pastry off the sheet, turn it over and return to the oven for 5 minutes or until golden and crisp. Transfer to a rack and leave to cool.

Whip the cream until thick and fold half into the custard. Reserve six whole cherries for decorating and stone and finely chop the rest. Fold the chopped cherries into the custard cream.

Cut the pastry lengthways into thirds, place one piece on a serving plate and spread with the cherry cream. Top with another piece of pastry, the remaining cherry cream and the remaining pastry. Pipe or spread the remaining whipped cream on top and decorate with the whole cherries. Cut into 6 slices to serve.

Saddle of Venison Cake

Rehrücken

So called because it is baked in a special *Rehrücken* mould to look like a saddle of venison, this cake is rich with chocolate and nuts.

---

4 oz/100g/½ cup unsalted butter, softened
4 oz/100g/¾ cup icing sugar
5 eggs, separated
2 oz/50g/½ cup ground almonds
2 oz/50g/1 cup fresh breadcrumbs
2 oz/50g plain chocolate, melted
1 tsp ground cinnamon
3 tbsp apricot jam
chocolate icing (see Viennese Nut Cake, p. 20)
about 8 whole blanched almonds, cut into sticks, to decorate
(serves about 8)

Pre-heat oven to gas mark 4/350°F/180°C. Beat the butter and sugar with an electric mixer until light and fluffy. Beat in the egg yolks, almonds, breadcrumbs, melted chocolate and cinnamon. Whisk the egg whites until stiff, then fold into the batter until evenly incorporated. Pour into a greased and floured 1¾ pint/1 litre/4½-cup *Rehrücken* mould or Balmoral cake tin and bake for 45 minutes or until a skewer inserted in the centre comes out clean. Invert onto a rack and leave to cool.

Melt the jam with 1½ tablespoons water, then work through a sieve and brush all over the cake. Pour the icing over the cake and press in the almond sticks. Leave to set before serving.

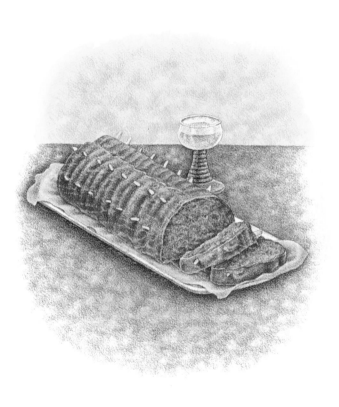

Cheesecake

Topfenkuchen

There are countless versions of *Topfenkuchen* to be found all over Austria, and *Topfen*, the Austrian equivalent of our cottage cheese, is widely used in Austrian baking. This traditional baked cheesecake is rich and sweet, and is especially good for morning coffee, served with *Schlagobers* (whipped cream).

Pastry:	Filling:
6 oz/150g/1 ½ cups plain flour	1 lb/450g/2 cups cottage cheese
pinch of salt	2 oz/50g/¼ cup caster sugar
3 oz/75g/⅓ cup unsalted butter, chilled	2 eggs, beaten
	4 oz/100g/¾ cup raisins
2 tbsp caster sugar	finely grated zest and juice of
finely grated zest of 1 lemon	1 lemon
1 egg, separated	

(serves 8)

To make the pastry: Sift the flour and salt into a bowl and work in the butter until the mixture resembles breadcrumbs. Stir in the sugar and lemon zest, then the egg yolk and enough water to bind the dough together. Form into a ball, then roll out on a floured surface and use to line a 7 in/18 cm springform tin. Brush with egg white and chill for 30 minutes.

Pre-heat oven to gas mark 4/350°F/180°C. Put all the filling ingredients in a bowl and beat well to mix. Pour into the pastry-lined tin and bake on a pre-heated baking sheet for 50 minutes or until the filling is set. Leave to cool in the tin before serving.

Index